My Bridal Shower

Name: _____

Date: _____

Peter Pauper Press, Inc.
White Plains, New York

By Evelyn L. Beilenson

Illustrated and designed by
Amy Dietrich

Printed on acid-free paper
Illustrations copyright © 2000
Amy Dietrich
Text copyright © 2000
Peter Pauper Press, Inc.
202 Mamaroneck Avenue
White Plains, NY 10601
ISBN 0-88088-648-X
Printed in China

7 6

Visit us at www.peterpauper.com

Contents

Who, When, and Where

Name of Bride:

Name of Groom:

Wedding Date:

Location:

Who, When, and Where

Shower given by:

Date and time:

Place:

Theme:

Who, When, and Where

place photo of bride
here

Who, When, and Where

place photo of bride and groom
here

Who, When, and Where

place photo of bridal party
here

8

The Scene

place photo
here

Invitation

place invitation
here

Menu

4-24-04
Kitchen Shower   Guest List

Kristin Rice
Kristen Butler
Christina LAdams
Wendy   Harris
Sarah Martin
Barbara Martin
Meta Adams
Vikki Locke
Laura diVer
Judy Rice

Guest List

Doris Pike

Susan Butler

Guest List

_____

_____

_____

_____

_____

_____

_____

_____

Guest List

_____

_____

_____

_____

_____

_____

_____

_____

Shower Gift Record

Gift	Given By

Shower Gift Record

Gift	Given By

Shower Gift Record

Gift	Given By

Shower Gift Record

Gift

Given By

Shower Gift Record

Gift	Given By

Shower Gift Record

Gift	Given By

Advice from Guests

Guest   Advice

Advice from Guests

Guest Advice

Advice from Guests

Guest   Advice

_____

_____

_____

_____

_____

_____

_____

Advice from Guests

Guest

Advice

Advice from Guests

Guest	Advice

Wisdom from Our Mothers

Advice from bride's mother: _____

_____

_____

_____

Advice from groom's mother: _____

_____

_____

_____

Shower Fun and Games

Shower Fun and Games

place photo
here

Special Moments

Special Moments

place photo
here

Shower Keepsakes

place flowers, ribbon,
napkins, etc.,
here

Shower Keepsakes

place flowers, ribbon,
napkins, etc.,
here

Scrapbook

News Events of the Day

Scrapbook

News Events of the Day

place news clippings
here

Bride's Thoughts

Bride's Thoughts

Groom's Thoughts

Groom's Thoughts

Photos

place photo
here

Photos

place photo
here

Photos

place photo
here

Photos

place photo
here

Photos

place photo
here

Photos

place photo
here

Photos

place photo
here

Photos

place photo
here

Photos

place photo
here

♥